ANCIENT AMERICAS

LIFE AMONG THE INCA

RACHEL STUCKEY

PowerKiDS press.
NEW YORK

Published in 2017 by **The Rosen Publishing Group, Inc.**
29 East 21st Street, New York, NY 10010

Developed and produced for Rosen by BlueAppleWorks Inc.

Art Director: Haley Harasymiw
Managing Editor for BlueAppleWorks: Melissa McClellan
Editor: Marcia Abramson
Design: T.J. Choleva

Picture credits: Cover: frgrd. LMspencer/Shutterstock; bkgrd. Michael Langford/Getty Images. Back cover: frgrd. Artishok/Shutterstock; bkgrd. altanaka/Shutterstock. Title page Helvetiker/Public Domain; p. 5 Sean Pathasema/Birmingham Museum of Art/Creative Commons; p. 7 Juan B. Lepiani/Public Domain; p. 7 inset Public Domain; p. 10 inset left Ondando/Creative Commons; p. 10 Martin St-Amant/Creative Commons; p. 1o inset right José Yépez A. /Public Domain; p. 11 left Rowanwindwhistler/Creative Commons; p. 11 A. Valdez/ Public Domain; p. 11 top right Daderot/Creative Commons; p. 11 bottom right Los Angeles County Museum of Art/Public Domain; p. 12 Fedekuki/Creative Commons; p. 15 Christian Vinces/Shutterstock; p. 15 bottom Neale Cousland/Shutterstock; p. 16 inset Yves Picq/Creative Commons; p. 16 Pedro Subercaseaux /Public Domain; p. 17 Iryna Savina/Shutterstock; p. 17 inset sunsinger/Shutterstock; p. 19 Atomart432/Creative Commons; p. 21 Vadim Petrakov/Shutterstock; p. 21 inset Agne Alminaite/Shutterstock; p. 22 Daderot/ Creative Commons; p. 24 inset left Lombards Museum/Creative Commons; p. 24 Jae/Creative Commons; p. 24 right jackf/Shutterstock; p. 25 left, 25 right Daderot /Public Domain; p. 25 elvetiker/Public Domain; p. 27 Julio Vila y Prades/Public Domain; p. 29, 29 bottom right Chris Howey/Shutterstock; p. 29 bottom left meunierd/Shutterstock; Maps: p. 9 T.J. Choleva/AridOcean/Shutterstock; p. 9 inset .J. Choleva/SoleilC/ Shutterstock

Cataloging-in-Publication Data
Names: Stuckey, Rachel.
Title: Life among the Inca / Rachel Stuckey.
Description: New York : PowerKids Press, 2017. | Series: Ancient Americas | Includes index.
Identifiers: ISBN 9781508149866 (pbk.) | ISBN 9781508149804 (library bound) | ISBN 9781508149682 (6 pack)
Subjects: LCSH: Incas--Juvenile literature. | Indians of South America--Juvenile literature.
Classification: LCC F3429.S78 2017| DDC 985'.019--dc23

Manufactured in the United States of America
CPSIA Compliance Information: Batch #BS16PK: For Further Information contact Rosen Publishing, New York, New York at 1-800-237-9932

CONTENTS

CHAPTER 1

THE INCA 4

CHAPTER 2

INCA EMPIRE 8

CHAPTER 3

INCA CITIES AND ARCHITECTURE . . 14

CHAPTER 4

LIFE IN THE INCA EMPIRE 18

CHAPTER 5

DOWNFALL AND LEGACY 26

GLOSSARY 30

FOR MORE INFORMATION 31

INDEX 32

CHAPTER 1

THE INCA

The Inca Empire stretched for 2,500 miles (4,023 km) from north to south along the western coast of South America, over the Andes Mountains and into the Amazon Rainforest. It covered around 380,000 square miles (984,195 square km) of territory. The Inca were expert engineers, building roads and **irrigation** systems that still impress modern researchers. They also ran their empire with great skill—collecting taxes, managing trade, and maintaining a huge army. But the empire lasted only 100 years before the Spanish **conquistadors** arrived.

A thousand years ago, there were many different groups or communities living in the Andes. Many of these groups spoke the Quechua language. Around A.D. 1200 a new group of Quechuan peoples moved into the Cusco valley of Peru. There they built a small kingdom centered around the city of Cusco. We don't know what these people called themselves then, but today we call them the Inca. For two hundred years, they lived quietly in their small city-state kingdom.

In 1438, a northern tribe called the Chancas attacked Cusco. Pachacutec, the son of Cusco's king, helped to defend the city and defeated the Chancas.

MANY INCA GOLD TREASURES, LIKE THIS CEREMONIAL KNIFE, HAVE BEEN FOUND, BUT LEGEND SAYS EVEN MORE ARE HIDDEN IN A SECRET INCA CAVE.

Pachacutec later claimed the throne and began to expand the kingdom to what is now Lima in the north and Lake Titicaca to the south. Pachacutec became the first Sapa Inca, or emperor. Twenty years later, he turned his army over to his son and then focused on organizing his government and administering his new empire. The emperors that followed expanded the territory north into Ecuador and south into Bolivia. The Inca called their empire *Tawantinsuyu*, which means "the four regions" or "four quarters." Cusco was the center of the empire with the four regions stretching north, south, east, and west.

SPANISH CONQUEST

In 1527 the Sapa Inca and his oldest son died from smallpox. Another son, Huascar, who lived in Cusco, claimed the throne. His brother Atahualpa, who lived in Quito, did not agree. A civil war began. In 1532, Atahualpa's forces defeated Huascar and Atahualpa claimed the throne in April.

What's in the name?

The Inca are not really the Inca. *Inka* means "ruler" or "lord" in Quechua. *Inka* was actually a title. When Pachacutec began building Tawantinsuyu, he was called *Sapa Inka*, which means "the only ruler." The Spanish conquistadors called Tawantinsuyu the *Imperio Inca* or Inca Empire, and soon "Inca" was used to identify all the subjects of the Sapa Inca.

BASED ON DRAWINGS MADE BY THE SPANISH, MANY ARTISTS HAVE DEPICTED ATAHUALPA (INSET) AND HIS CAPTURE.

But civil war had made the empire weak and disorganized. Spanish conquistadors led by Francisco Pizarro were able to take cities throughout the empire.

The new Sapa Inca Atahualpa believed the small Spanish force of around 160 men was no match for his 80,000 warriors, so he invited the Spanish to the town of Cajamarca. But, the Spanish launched a surprise attack in the town square using their cannons and men on horseback. They captured Atahualpa and killed 500 Inca warriors. Not a single conquistador died. Pizarro used Atahualpa to control the empire at first, but later executed him. He founded a Spanish capital in Lima and within a year the Inca Empire was defeated.

CHAPTER 2

INCA EMPIRE

The Inca Empire had a very strict political and social structure. The Sapa Inca Pachacutec and his family were at the top. Below the Sapa Inca were the high priest and the commander-in-chief of the army. There was also a council of powerful **nobles** who advised the Sapa Inca and each quarter of the empire had its own leader called an *apu*.

A large middle class helped the Sapa Inca administer the empire. Inspectors made sure people paid their taxes and followed the rules. The middle class also included engineers, architects, and accountants. There were also regional army commanders or generals. The next class down included craftsmen, musicians, and army captains. The lowest class included the farmers, shepherds, and workmen or builders.

The government was centered in Cusco, which was also the religious center of the empire. But the Inca allowed the people they conquered to worship their own gods alongside the Incan gods. They also put a local person in charge and gave them control of small local issues. This made it easier for Cusco to control the diverse population of the empire and keep the conquered people happy.

THE INCA EMPIRE GREW TO BECOME THE LARGEST IN THE AMERICAS.

THE INCA ARMY USED A VAST NETWORK OF ROADS THAT CROSSED MANY OBSTACLES. WORKERS CARVED ROADS INTO MOUNTAINSIDES AND BUILT ROPE BRIDGES ACROSS GORGES.

MILITARY MIGHT

The Inca had an army of fierce, well-trained warriors. With his large army, the Sapa Inca was able to protect against threats and increase his territory. The Inca often used their military strength as a **diplomatic** strategy. Because the army was so big, rivals often surrendered before the battle even began.

The army also traveled quickly throughout the empire along the Inca Road. The government kept storehouses of food called *tambos* along the roads. This made it easy for the commanders to feed the army, even on long marches. So the army was always well prepared when it arrived at its destination.

TRADE AND TAXES

The Inca traded mostly within the empire. While they are famous for their gold and silver, they did not use this resource for trade. In fact, there was no money in the empire. Instead, food and handmade goods like textiles were traded between communities. And the government controlled all long-distance trade within the empire.

To manage trade and keep the empire going, the Sapa Inca collected two types of taxes: goods and labor. The first type of tax was paid with crops or handmade goods. Each community or *ayllu* gave a portion of its crops to the empire. One third of all crops were paid to the government, one third to the priests, and one third was kept by the people.

THE INCA WOVE BASKETS FOR STORING AND TRANSPORTING FOOD. HANDMADE POTTERY WAS USED FOR COOKING AND SERVING.

RECORDS TIED UP IN KNOTS

The Inca did not have a writing system. Instead, they used a special tool for record keeping called a *quipu*. A quipu was a collection of strings with knots. The size of the knots, how they were spaced, and the number of knots all had meaning. The accountants who used the quipus were called *quipucamayoc*. Managing this system took very special training and the quipucamayoc held an important position in Incan society—much like scribes in other civilizations.

When farmers were not tending their crops, they paid their labor tax. This was called the *mit'a*. To pay the *mit'a*, every man in the lower classes either built and maintained roads and buildings, worked in the silver and gold mines, or served in the army. The tax inspectors made sure that everyone paid what they owed. They also made sure that everyone in the empire followed the rules laid out by the government in Cusco.

THE INCA ROAD

The Inca Empire had a system of roads that was 24,000 miles (39,000 km) long and connected every community within the empire. The Inca did not build all of the roads—the groups and civilizations that came before them began building the roads hundreds of years earlier. But the Inca expanded the roads, improved them, and created a network that led back to Cusco from all corners of the empire.

The Inca roads are impressive examples of engineering. They were built entirely by hand without any metal tools, draft animals, or wheeled transportation. The roads stood up to earthquakes and water **erosion** better than the roads we build today.

Commoners were not allowed to use the roads. The government controlled them for communication, transportation of goods, and moving the army. Very fast runners worked as messengers or *chaskis*. A chaski would run at top speed to a relay station and pass on a verbal message or a *quipu* to the next runner. Using this method, a message could travel around 250 miles (402 km) a day.

While the roads helped the Inca control their empire, they also helped the Spanish conquer it. It was easy for the Spanish to get from Cusco to the rest of the empire. And because the Spanish only cared about the gold and silver mines, many of the roads were left to crumble. But after 500 years of neglect, many parts of the roads still exist. These foot trails connect communities throughout the Andes Mountains.

Hiking the Inca Trail

You can trek the Inca Road today. The most popular trek is part of the road from Cusco to Machu Picchu. Known as the Inca Trail, this 26-mile (42-km) trek takes 4 days and reaches elevations of over 13,000 feet (4000 m). Inca Trail hikers must obtain a government permit and hire a guide.

CHAPTER 3

INCA CITIES AND ARCHITECTURE

The Inca had several methods of construction and building design. But they are most remembered for their **dry stone** work. The Inca could cut and fit large stones together without using **mortar**. Some of these walls still stand—the stones fit together so tightly, a knife cannot slide between them. Researchers are not sure where they **quarried** the stone to build their great temples and palaces with this technique. But building techniques were different depending on the region. Near the coast, the Inca used **adobe** bricks. And in the mountains, they used **fieldstones** and mortar to build walls and roads.

ALL ROADS LEAD TO CUSCO

The city of Cusco was the center of the Incan world, sitting at 11,200 feet (3,400 m) above sea level. When Pachacutec became the Sapa Inca, he started to rebuild and expand the city. According to legend, the city was laid out in the shape of a reclining mountain lion or puma.

Just outside the city, the great temple complex and fortress of Sacsayhuaman was the puma's head. Sacsayhuaman was first built by the Killke people who lived in Cusco before the Inca arrived in A.D. 1200.

PEOPLE TODAY STILL MARVEL AT THE INTACT WALLS OF SACSAYHUAMAN.

AFTER CONQUERING CUSCO, THE SPANISH BUILT A CHURCH OVER THE CORICANCHA, BUT SOME ORIGINAL WALLS STILL ARE VISIBLE (INSET).

Pachacutec began expanding the original fortress into a great temple pyramid around 1440. It took 50 years and 20,000 workers to complete. Some of the dry stone walls reached 13 feet (4 m) high.

The Coricancha or "gold enclosure" was in the heart of the city. Dedicated to the sun god Inti, Coricancha had walls covered in gold. The temple was full of golden statues and a large gold disc represented Inti.

MACHU PICCHU

Machu Picchu is the most famous example of Incan architecture. Because the Spanish never occupied the site, what we see today is completely Incan. Some archaeologists believe it was a vacation retreat for the Sapa Inca, as it is a beautiful site and warmer than Cusco. Others think it was a sacred religious site.

Machu Picchu is not very big—only around 1,000 nobles, priests, and servants could live there. There are around 140 buildings and 100 stairways in Machu Picchu. Archaeologists have also discovered an underground irrigation system that controlled the flow of water into fountains that still work today.

The Inca began building Machu Picchu under Sapa Inca Pachacutec in 1450. Construction continued until the Spanish Conquest, but then Machu Picchu was abandoned. Some peasants lived in the buildings and farmed the fields, but despite this, the site was basically lost for four hundred years. In 1911 the explorer Hiram Bingham was led there by a local boy. Bingham cleared the overgrown vegetation and documented the site. In 1948 Bingham published a book about his discovery called *The Lost City of the Incas*, introducing Machu Picchu to the world.

WHILE MACHU PICCHU LOOKS LIKE A CITY IN THE SKY, IT IS ONLY 8,000 FEET (2,400 M) ABOVE SEA LEVEL—MUCH LOWER THAN CUSCO.

CHAPTER 4

LIFE IN THE INCA EMPIRE

Inca society was made up of *ayllu*, groups of families that lived and worked together. Men were married by the age of 20, and women married between the ages of 12 and 16. Noblemen could have many wives, but commoners could only marry one woman.

Most of the men in the empire were farmers. They worked the land owned by the Sapa Inca, growing food for their family and to pay their taxes to the empire. From the age of 16, Inca men had to contribute labor to the empire to pay their *mit'a* or labor tax. For part of the year they worked constructing buildings and roads, mining gold or silver, or serving in the army.

Women worked in the home all day. They prepared food, cared for children, and made clothing. Women also wove textiles from wool and cotton. Inca women from all classes were skilled weavers. The best weavers in the empire were taken to live in Cusco to produce cloth for the nobility and the army.

FARMING

The Inca knew how to farm in the many different conditions found throughout the empire. They grew crops in the jungle and on the coast.

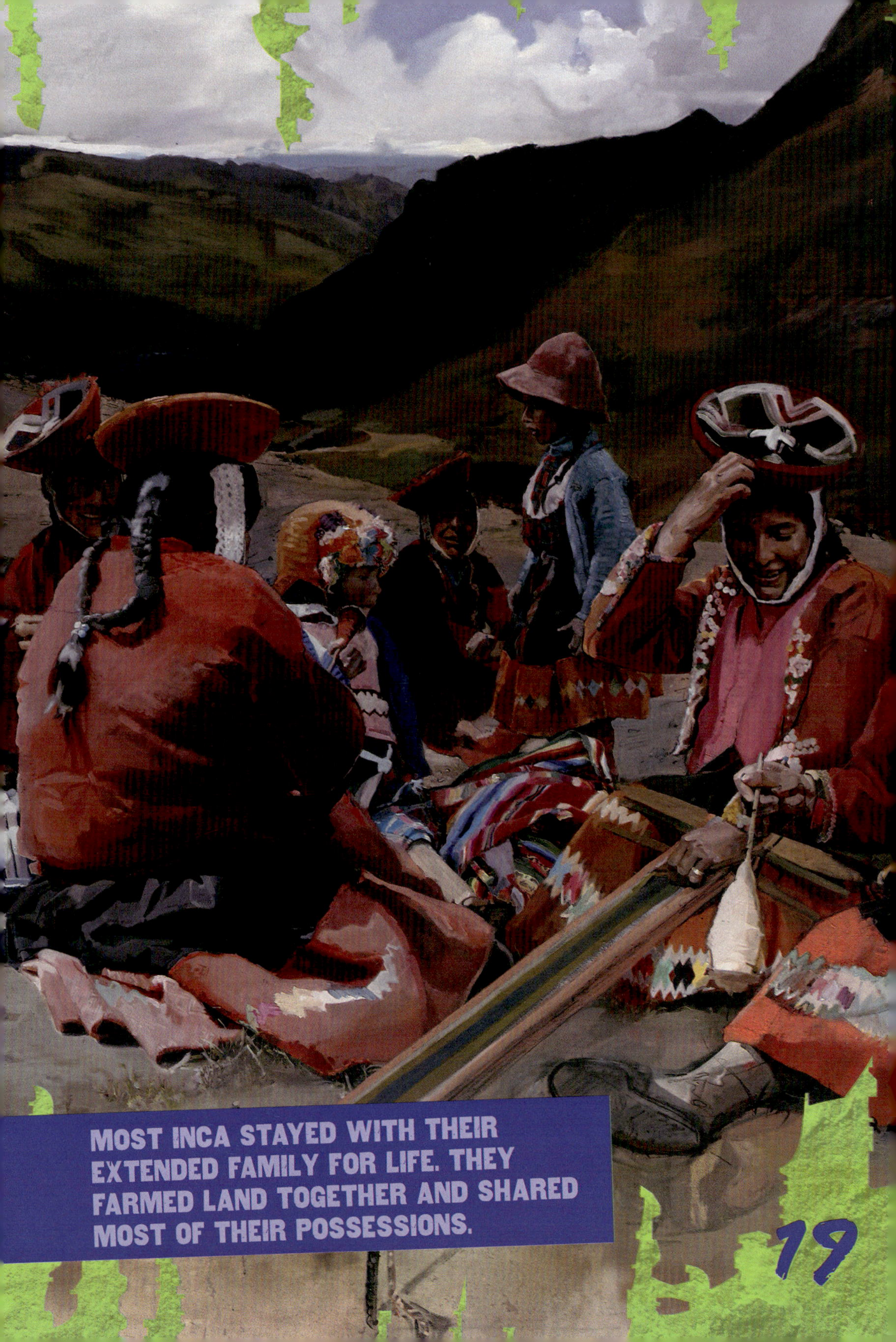

MOST INCA STAYED WITH THEIR EXTENDED FAMILY FOR LIFE. THEY FARMED LAND TOGETHER AND SHARED MOST OF THEIR POSSESSIONS.

COCA LEAF

One of the most important crops in the Incan world wasn't used for food. The coca plant is a natural stimulant that was used as medicine and for religious rituals. The plant has been part of Andean culture for thousands of years. The plant can be used to make the illegal drug cocaine, but today people in the Andes chew the leaf and brew coca tea for energy and to prevent altitude sickness. Inca men carried a small bag of coca leaves for chewing.

But they also used irrigation to grow crops in the desert and the high mountains. They built cisterns to capture and store rainwater, and built canals that brought water down the mountains.

The Inca built stone **terraces** to create flat land for farming in the mountains. At the height of the empire, there were 2.5 million acres (1 million hectares) of terraces. Like the Inca roads, the terraces were engineering marvels. Researchers today believe that Inca terraces are the most sophisticated in the world. The terraces retained enough water for the crops but drained excess water to keep the walls from collapsing.

Potatoes

Potatoes come from South America. The Incas' ancestors were the first to cultivate them. Now farmers grow 4,000 kinds of potatoes in the Andes!

IN MANY PARTS OF PERU, INCA TERRACES ARE SO WELL BUILT THAT LOCAL FARMERS CONTINUE TO USE THEM TODAY.

The stone walls also retained heat from the sun to keep roots warm on cold mountain nights. This allowed the Inca to extend their growing season.

RELIGION AND WORSHIP

Religion was an important part of Incan life. The Sapa Inca was considered a god, which made religion a part of the imperial government. Inti was the god of the sun and the most important god. The Sapa Inca was believed to be a descendant of Inti. Mama Quilla was the goddess of the moon and Pachamama was the goddess of the earth, or Mother Earth. Viracocha was the creator of all things and Supay was the god of death.

The Inca believed in the **afterlife**. They **embalmed** and **mummified** bodies before burial and brought gifts for the dead to use in the afterlife. The mummified emperor was kept in the palace and included as part of religious festivals. There were festivals every month. The Inca also practiced **human sacrifice**, or the ritual killing of people to honor the gods.

The Inca believed that spirits could inhabit any object or place. A *huaca* was an object that contained a spirit. It could be human made, like a stone altar, or natural, like a waterfall. The Inca prayed to the huaca and offered sacrifices. Even a mummy could be a huaca. The most sacred huaca were the mummified bodies of the emperors. There were huaca all along the Inca Road, such as stone altars to Pachamama and Inti.

AFTER MUMMIFYING THEIR DEAD, THE INCA SENT THEM TO THE AFTERLIFE WITH JEWELRY, POTTERY, TEXTILES, AND EVEN SANDALS.

CAPACCOCHA – HONORING THE GODS

The Incan practice of human sacrifice was called *qhapaq hucha* in Quechua, which means "solemn sacrifice." The Spanish called the practice **capaccocha**. The purpose was to honor the gods by sending them the best Inca. The most beautiful and physically perfect children were offered to the gods and killed in a ritual sacrifice. In 1954 the remains of a mummified child were discovered on the Cerro El Plomo mountain, in Chile. It was the first high-altitude mummy ever discovered. It also provided evidence of the Incan practice of capaccocha.

THE ASTRONOMERS

The Inca had a calendar based on the sun's position in the sky. The Inca used their calendar to track the seasons for planting and harvesting. They also tracked their many religious festivals. The Incan year had 12 months and each month had three weeks of 10 days each. The Inca added extra days to align their calendar with the solar year, which is 365 days.

The Inca were also **astronomers**. The rising and setting of the sun, moon, and stars were important events. For example, the Incan New Year began when the Pleiades star cluster rose. They also built pillars on the hills outside Cusco—when the sun rose and set between the pillars it was time to plant. Different sets of pillars identified the planting times for different parts of the empire—the coast, the lowlands, the jungle, the valleys, and the mountains. The Inca also built **observatories** throughout the empire. The most important observatory was the Coricancha sun temple in Cusco.

TEXTILES WERE PRIZED BY THE INCAS. THEY WERE WOVEN WITH WOOL FROM LLAMAS (RIGHT) AND THEIR SMALLER ALPACA AND VICUÑA COUSINS.

ARTS AND CULTURE

In Incan society, architects and engineers were part of the public administration class. They were higher in class than artisans or craftsmen, who were commoners. But artisans and craftsmen did not have to pay the *mit'a* labor tax, and the government paid them with the food from the farmers' taxes.

The most important Incan art was textiles. Weaving was very important in Incan society—weavers were buried with their tools. The Inca textiles were made using cotton on the coast and in the lowlands. In the mountains they used the wool of **llama**, **alpaca**, and **vicuña**. The vicuña wool was for the royal family only.

There were three types of cloth. *Chusi* was rough and used for blankets. The everyday cloth was called *awasca*. The finest cloth was called *qompi*. The textiles had many intricate designs. The Spanish burned many textiles, but some cloth from the empire still survives. Inca designs also were recorded in Spanish drawings. And the people of the Andes continued to use Incan designs long after the fall of the empire.

The Inca also used gold and silver for many things such as making jewelry and decorating temples. The Sapa Inca even had a throne made of solid gold. Unfortunately, the Spanish melted down most of the Inca gold and silver metalwork.

MANY INCA TREASURES WERE TAKEN OUT OF SOUTH AMERICA AND ENDED UP IN MUSEUMS ALL OVER THE WORLD. IN RECENT YEARS, SOME HAVE BEEN GIVEN BACK TO PERU.

CHAPTER 5

DOWNFALL AND LEGACY

One hundred years after Pachacutec began the empire, it started to crumble. In the early 1500s, a smallpox epidemic killed 200,000 Incas and weakened the rest. When the Sapa Inca died in 1527 from smallpox, his sons fought for the throne in a five-year civil war. The civil war weakened the empire and distracted the Incan armies.

The Spanish conquistador Francisco Pizarro was serving as the royal governor of the newly conquered Panama. He first encountered Incan power and wealth when he visited the northern city of Tumbes in 1528. He believed that finding and conquering the Incan capital of Cusco would make him a rich man. He returned to Spain to get royal permission to conquer South America. The king and queen of Spain made a deal that one fifth of whatever they found in South America would go to the crown, and the conquistadors could keep the rest.

Pizarro began his **expedition** into Incan territory with about 160 men and 60 horses. Pizarro was surprised to find the cities in ruins from the civil war. Pizarro and his men began their march toward Cusco. The weakened Inca did not adapt their military strategy to defend against the Spanish weapons and horses.

FRANCISCO PIZARRO, A BRUTAL CONQUEROR, WAS KILLED IN A FEUD WITH OTHER SPANIARDS WHEN HE WAS ABOUT 70. HE WAS BURIED IN LIMA.

ROOM FILLED WITH GOLD

When the Spanish captured Sapa Inca Atahualpa, he promised them a room filled with gold and silver as ransom. The Spanish were shocked, but the Sapa Inca's subjects brought more gold and silver every day—13,000 pounds (5,900 kg) of gold and twice as much silver. But fearing an Incan uprising, the Spanish executed the Sapa Inca anyway. Some of the Incan nobility and generals retreated. They named a new Sapa Inca and fought back against the conquistadors for many years. But in the end, they could not overcome Spanish power.

While the Inca were fierce warriors they often fell apart without their leaders. The Spanish took advantage of this. When the new Sapa Inca came to meet the Spanish in the town square of Cajamarca, they went straight for him and took him captive. By 1533, Pizarro and his men had conquered Cusco and looted the city. Pizarro ruled as governor of Peru until his death in 1541.

LEGACY

Half of the Inca died soon after the Spanish Conquest, most from diseases carried by the Spanish. Many of the roads, water systems, and terraces were abandoned. Because the Spanish enforced their own methods of farming and building, much of the Incan knowledge was lost. Much of Cusco's Incan architecture was lost during the Spanish Conquest. Conquistadors looted the city of its gold and silver and then built over the Incan temples and buildings. Today the Church of Santo Domingo stands on the site of the Coricancha.

However, the people in the Andes still speak Quechua. And many mountain communities still live the way their Incan ancestors did. They weave their own cloth, walk the old roads from town to town, and chew coca leaf and drink coca tea.

There are Incan ruins in many of the countries of South America but most of them are found near Cusco. Over a million tourists visit this part of Peru every year. Today Andean communities are trying to bring Incan technology back to life, rebuilding the terraces and irrigation systems to develop modern **sustainable** farming.

PERU CELEBRATES ITS INCA HERITAGE BY RECREATING FESTIVALS SUCH AS INTI RAYMI, HONORING THE SUN GOD. THE ANNUAL EVENT IS HELD AT SACSAYHUAMAN.

GLOSSARY

adobe: a type of clay that can be dried into bricks in the sun

afterlife: life after death

alpaca: a long-haired mammal in the camel family

astronomer: a person that studies planets and stars in space

capaccocha: the Incan practice of human sacrifice of children

commoners: the lower classes of a society, anyone who is not a member of the nobility or descendant of royalty

conquistadors: the explorers and soldiers sent by Spain to conquer the New World

diplomatic: using negotiation to reach agreements between countries

dry stone: made by cutting and fitting large stones together without using mortar

embalm: to preserve a body

erosion: when something gradually wears away, usually from wind and water

expedition: a journey taken by a group of people usually for exploration

fieldstone: stone used in its natural form

human sacrifice: the killing of a person in a religious ritual to honor a god

irrigation: supplying land with water through canals or pipes

llama: a long-haired mammal in the camel family

mortar: a mixture of material that hardens when it dries, used to hold bricks or stones together

mummify: to preserve a body by embalming and wrapping in cloth

nobles: a group of people at the top of a society, usually with inherited titles and related to the royal family

observatories: buildings used for studying the sky

quarried: mined stones from the ground

subjects: citizens of a nation ruled by a king or queen

sustainable: able to be repeated without using up resources

terraces: a flat area created on a slope using walls

vicuña: a wild llama with very fine wool

FOR MORE INFORMATION

BOOKS

DK Publishing. *Aztec, Inca & Maya*. New York: DK Eyewitness Books, 2011.

Garbe, Suzanne. *Secrets of Machu Picchu: Lost City of the Incas*. Mankato, MN: Capstone Press, 2014.

Kovacs, Lawrence. *Inca: Discover the Culture and Geography of a Lost Civilization*. White River Junction, VT: Nomad Press, 2013.

WEBSITES

Due to the changing nature of Internet links, PowerKids Press has developed an online list of websites related to the subject of this book. This site is updated regularly. Please use this link to access the list:

www.powerkidslinks.com/aa/inca

INDEX

A
Andes Mountains 4, 13, 20, 25, 29
Atahualpa 6, 7, 28

B
Bingham, Hiram 17

C
Cajamarca 7, 9, 28
calendar 23
capaccocha 23
Chancas 4
coca leaf 20, 29
Cusco 4, 6, 8, 9, 12, 13, 14, 16, 17, 18, 23, 26, 28, 29

G
gold 11, 12, 13, 16, 18, 25, 28

H
Huascar 6

I
Inca Road 10, 12, 13, 22
Incan ruins 29
irrigation systems 4, 29

L
llamas 24

M
Machu Picchu 9, 13, 16, 17
military 10, 26

P
Pachacutec 4, 6, 8, 14, 16, 17, 26
Panama 9, 26
Peru 4, 9, 21, 25, 28, 29
Pizarro, Francisco 7, 26, 27

Q
Quechua language 4, 6, 23, 29
quipu 12, 13

S
Sapa Inca 6, 7, 8, 10, 11, 14, 16, 17, 18, 21, 25, 26, 28
South America 4, 9, 20, 25, 26, 29
Spanish conquest 6, 17, 28
Spanish conquistadors 4, 6, 7

T
taxes 4, 8, 11, 18, 24
terraces 20, 21, 28, 29

W
warriors 7, 10, 28
weavers 18, 24